SLA GUIDELINES

From Audiobooks to E-books

Alternative Formats to Engage Non-readers

Eileen Armstrong and Sally Duncan

Series Editor: Geoff Dubber

School Library Association

Acknowledgements

The SLA Publications Team would like to thank Cathy Wright from New College, Worcester (the national residential school and college for young people aged 11 to 19 who are blind or partially sighted), who put some initial ideas together for this publication back in 2005! We would also like to thank Moira Johnson and Juliet Leeves from Treloar College, Alton, Hampshire (a specialist college for young people aged 16 and over with physical disabilities), Shona Phillips, previously at the Royal Blind School Edinburgh, now working at Edinburgh Academy and also Claire Larson of Hursthead Junior School, Stockport, for their very useful case studies. Special thanks are due to SLA ex-Chair and reading aficionado Eileen Armstrong who produced the greater part of the excellent text with the help of our own Sally Duncan and thanks also to Chris Brown who gave us words of wisdom. Many of us had a hand in this publication, not least Richard Leveridge and Jane Cooper who did much of the behind the scenes work with it… thank you to everyone.

Published by

School Library Association
1 Pine Court, Kembrey Park
Swindon
SN2 8AD

Tel: 01793 530166   Fax: 01793 481182
E-mail: info@sla.org.uk
Web: www.sla.org.uk

Registered Charity No: 313660
Charity Registered in Scotland No: SC039453

Cover photographs by Martin Salter
Printed by Printondemand-Worldwide

Contents

Introduction   3

Alternative Formats   6

Book and Author Promotion Websites   11

Reading Promotion Websites   20

Where to go for Resources   27

Library Suppliers   38

Case Studies

Information Access for All at Treloar College   40

School Library Provision for Children and
Young People with Special Needs   47

Using E-readers for a Book Group at a Junior School   50

Appendix One

Other Sources of Advice   55

> *Fewer than 5% of children's books are commercially available in alternative formats, such as large print, audio or Braille but there are 25,000 children in the UK with a visual impairment.*
>
> — Carolyn Fullard, Chief Executive, National Blind Children's Society. July 2009

> *When you read often and with enthusiasm, usually just for the sheer fun of it, you lay foundations that last for life. You empathise. You access information more easily. Almost by osmosis you internalise the essential skills of spelling, grammar and vocabulary. You learn to express yourself verbally and in writing. You learn to interpret and potentially change your world.*
>
> —Alan Gibbons *Reading 4 Pleasure*. NUT, 2012

Please note:

The hardware and software for audiobooks and e-books is a fast-evolving field but this Guideline has aimed to be up-to-date at the time of publication.

The legal requirements for the use and loan of audiobooks, e-books and e-readers in libraries vary, so please consult the terms and conditions of your supplier. For further information, see the e-resources page in the Support for Secondary Schools section of the SLA website: http://www.sla.org.uk/eresources.php

There's more than one way to read a book or indeed any kind of text. Most of us, especially those of us working in libraries, take for granted the reading process – we pick up a book and read it without really noticing what we are doing. We are able to take in big chunks of a page at once, we are able to skip through passages to look for particular words, and quickly go back to earlier parts of the text to see if we have missed anything, or to reread what we feel we didn't understand.

Some people read in an entirely different way, however, and these people access books by using alternative formats – that is, alternative to standard print. One group of these are people with a visual impairment, but there are many others – young people with dyslexia, for instance, or those for whom reading is a struggle. The process is just too challenging to allow the magic and power of the story to come through. Add to this people who find holding a book physically hard work, maybe through illness or as the result of an accident, and you find quite a variety of potential readers who would appreciate the opportunity to read a book in an alternative way. An increasing number of young people simply do not enjoy reading traditional print. Alternative formats open a door to a rich, vital and energising world that most of us take for granted. They are also, increasingly, a new and exciting way to bring story to a generation of digital natives. A tool librarians can use to create readers.

Reading books in alternative formats is quite a different technique from reading in standard print. If you are a touch reader and you read in Braille, you can only read a tiny bit of text at a time, maybe only one letter or one syllable. Skimming and scanning can be more challenging and if you are trying to find the place in a book where you got to last time, you have to read a whole chunk one word at a time till you get to the place you are looking for. Similarly, if you read books using cassettes you can only go through the story in one way – from beginning to end. CDs likewise, but as tracks are bookmarked it is easier to find a particular place. Or you might read books in print, but can only see a small part of the page at one time, so that you, too, cannot quickly scan a page to find the right place or a particular word. You might quite simply prefer a more visual presentation such as a graphic novel. Digital books too offer a whole new way of experiencing narrative – not necessarily sequentially.

The school librarian, therefore, when trying to hook these young people into reading has to sometimes overcome not only physical or cognitive barriers but a real reluctance, a fear of failure and strong sense that reading is not for them as well.

A critic might well ask, why bother to encourage young people to read when entertainment through many different channels in the mass media is readily available? Surely this is just the natural evolution of communication and we should just accept that reading is going to be less popular and universal in the future? I would argue that the power of narrative is even stronger in this context. Young people who are able to access the magic of story find benefits both intellectually and psychologically – intellectually through the absorption of powerful and varied use of language which will positively impact on their own skill with words, and psychologically through the vicarious experiences which a story offers. Stories allow the young reader to access new worlds and experiences, to rehearse situations, and to try things out through characters in books which in reality would be too risky. Young people with some form of text impairment perhaps have even more to gain from the life-saving window on the world that a powerful story has to offer, as their life experiences may be limited yet their need for social wisdom and experience is just as great as for anyone else.

In providing texts for this special group of young people, particularly those in the 11–16 age range, the librarian can exploit the many different formats and types of media available these days. A student will often accept a story when it is presented as a DVD or an audio book rather than in print, and there are many different ways of accessing texts electronically these days.

Dedicated e-reading devices such as the Amazon Kindle, Kobo, Nook and the Sony e-reader have proved immensely popular and whilst early adopters were undoubtedly gadgetophile males the devices are rapidly taking off with older readers and changing the family demographic of reading. The speculation is that parents will hand down their devices to younger children as new models become available and indeed much of the most exciting e-book development is in picture books and apps for the very youngest by new and innovative publishers such as Nosy Crow (http://nosycrow.com/apps/). Rapidly increasing ownership of these devices over the last two years, together with the rise in smartphone and tablet technology has now pushed digital reading firmly into the mainstream.

Research carried out by Bowker showed that only 14% of reading teens regularly read digitally. In many respects the UK seems to be trailing behind the rest of the world in e-book provision. One likely influence on what happens next is the extent to which the education sector adopts e-reading devices. American and Australasian school libraries have already embedded e-book lending into their provision, Taiwan has launched the 'e-schoolbags' programme using iPads and e-learning devices and the Catalonian government has decreed that all textbooks must be supplied digitally. This is an exciting time for school librarians who could easily become pioneers in the digital revolution.

Handheld e-reading devices have also proved to be a surefire way to hook in reluctant male teenagers (see Lancaster, Adam (2012). *Showing Impact: Mapping and Tracking Students' Reading in the Secondary School Library*. SLA Voices. 978-1-903446-67-6). A number of small-scale pilot e-reader projects in UK schools have shown a stunning increase in reading engagement and achievement. The advent of the iPod Touch, iPhone and, more recently, the iPad4, can only accelerate the number of e-books and book apps available and transform what we understand by the reading experience.

In print, there are some good versions of classic stories presented in condensed forms and the presentation of some books using carefully chosen fonts and paper makes them readily accessible to all readers. Additionally, the group of young people who have physical or sensory but not necessarily psychological barriers to reading might also be hungry for books they can access.

Check out this book's forthcoming sister publication *Riveting Reads: Alternative Formats* for loads of suggested titles to engage these readers.

With so many formats available now more young people are able to read more in many more ways and in ways which suit them – and that can only be a good thing!

Alternative Formats

What kinds of alternative formats are there?

You can read using your eyes, your ears or your fingers. Many people choose a combination of methods depending on the task, or on other factors including how tired they are, or the lighting environment in the room.

Audio formats

Some people prefer to access books using audio after reading the text, others prefer to start with the audio version or to read the two simultaneously for support. Many students who find reading difficult benefit from listening to the story while following the text. Publishers are increasingly providing CDs or audiofiles to accompany their series for struggling readers, e.g. Rising Stars and Badger Learning. Listening to the text first can prepare the reader for the hard copy text to follow. Familiarity with the plot, characters, locations and proper names can be a real boon for some readers.

A visually impaired reader might have speech synthesis software on their computer which would enable them to listen to any computer file. However, these just use a synthesised computer voice (which have improved immeasurably over recent years so that they now sound more like something out of *Desperate Housewives* rather than a dalek), but even though these may be very good for school work or reference, they are hardly the kind of thing to curl up with for a good story!

Ordinary, commercially produced cassettes/CDs using professional actors, and more frequently these days, MP3 files, are the best ways for people to access stories. Incidentally, the students at a school for the visually impaired in Scotland prefer unabridged to abridged versions, and they like fully dramatised stories best of all.

Pre-loaded, all-in-one, ready-to-listen digital audiobooks are now available via Audiogo and are well received by children and young people for their 'gadget factor'. Smaller than a pack of cards you simply plug in the headphones and start listening. It is possible to bookmark favourite bits, start listening again where you left off and control the speed of narration. Playaways are designed and sold for library use. (http://www.bbcaudiobooks.com/libraries/)

Obviously you don't have to have a visual impairment or reading difficulty to enjoy an audio story. There are few of us who don't enjoy being read to, so a good audio collection is an important part of any school library stock.

Print

There are many different kinds of print – an obvious statement but one which can be significant when trying to get a young person hooked on books. Close, small print in a font such as Times New Roman on a bright white paper can be really daunting and the reflection from bright paper can make it surprisingly difficult to read. Some publishers, such as Barrington Stoke, take care to use a more easily readable, slightly larger font, the paper is a pleasingly opaque cream colour and lines are widely spaced and not justified – another way in which readability is improved.

In terms of illustration, every reader is different and some will be attracted to bright design and imaginative graphics, while for others pictures and text in unpredictable places on the page will just make the book more difficult to read. This would probably apply to children with visual impairments and those with dyslexia, whilst students with short attention spans may be more likely to appreciate imaginative and unpredictable design.

There are very few publishers who produce large print books for children but one – the National Blind Children's Society (www.nbcs.org.uk) – does customised books, where the reader specifies the font and size, as well as the colour of the paper used. The books are for sale, and the registered blind or partially sighted customer pays the retail price – exactly the same price as a sighted customer would pay in a bookshop. Other customers pay a price per page, so the larger the print the more expensive the book.

For some students with visual impairment, or even dyslexia, many schools are forced to produce resources themselves as a result of the paucity of published large print texts – when this happens it is worth trying paper in one or two different colours – a pastel yellow or blue, for instance can be easier to read than bright white copier paper.

Another factor, if a school is binding their own material, is that a spiral binding enables the student to put the book flat on the desk or reading stand and if necessary use a magnifier with it.

Students with impaired vision or who experience difficulty with text can often benefit from the use of a CCTV. This is in fact close-circuit television – a small camera is located above a reading platform which then magnifies the page onto a computer screen. They are available in desktop or laptop versions and they enable many readers to access a much larger range of texts.

Braille

Braille is a system of raised dots. The system works on a pattern of six dots rather like a (very small) egg box called a cell. It's a code where one sign (one combination of the six dots) stands for one letter, and there are also signs which stand for either whole words or combinations of letters, such as 'ing', 'st' and so on.

The school librarian can support the Braille reader alongside the specialist teachers and other professionals. Books can be borrowed free from the National Library for the Blind (www.rnib.org.uk) and a long term loan arrangement allows the librarian to have a range of books on the shelf for the reader to browse and choose.

Braille readers range from extremely fluent, competent and literate, to those who are learning to use the medium and might need lots of encouragement and immediate success.

Braille readers can now access electronic titles by means of 'refreshable Braille' – a magnetic strip which displays a moving line of Braille as the cursor moves up and down. This means that any text which is available in an electronic format can be read in Braille either on a Braille strip attached to a standard desk or lap top computer, or on a Braille note taker device, of which there are several on the market.

Digital formats

One of the most popular and fast-developing formats is digital. Many young people have MP3 players, iPods or iPhones and for some it is much more 'cool' to be seen with one of these than an old fashioned book! Digital books allow adjustment of brightness and contrast of the page as well as adjustable print size making them a useful format for those with a visual impairment. It is a useful format for challenged or reluctant readers – those who would enjoy a good story but wouldn't be seen dead in the school library or with a book. As well as the huge range of music available there is an increasing choice of audio books on the Internet which can be downloaded onto portable, increasingly multifunctional, devices. The downside is that as far as libraries in the UK go, this trade is in its infancy with licensing and copyright issues yet to be worked out. By and large, you can buy an audio book from a company such as audible.com as an individual customer and download it onto your own portable player, but no agreements are yet in place for a library to purchase a title and lend it out to readers. This is a development that has already taken place in other countries such as the United States where Amazon have recently announced their intention to lend Kindle books through public libraries, so I'm sure it won't be long before it becomes possible here. Many UK public libraries are developing their e-book offer through providers such as OverDrive (www.overdrive.com) and Wheelers (www.wheelers.co.nz/info/ebooks) and it is worth promoting their availability to students.

There is an increasing number of e-books on the market to download, or to obtain for free. Increasingly publishers are making the first book in a series available free to download to increase or reinvigorate interest when a new title is published: *The Secret Life of Tanner Bree, Vampirates, Skulduggery Pleasant, Vampire Diaries*, the *Gone* novels. This format will tempt not only those who want a new gadget but also those who need something more than the traditional page to turn. Many public library services now offer e-books through OverDrive and Bloomsbury are experimenting with a 'Bookshelf' of titles on a subscription basis also available to school libraries. The advent of the iPad and i-Bookstore has led to a massive interest in e-book publishing.

Specially designed apps have added interactive functionality to involve the reader in telling the story and bringing the story vividly to life. The Costa prize-winning *Maggot Moon* is also available as an interactive book, bringing the story to life in a whole new way. Interactive content includes a video interview with Sally Gardner, extracts from the audiobook, discussion points and animated page sequences which allow the reader to see what a page looks like, and how reading feels, to a dyslexic.

According to BookScan, print book sales in 2012 are now running at a nine-year low, with sales down 11% year on year. Conversely digital formats now account for around 20% of publisher revenue showing that spending has moved to e-books rather than print. Adult fiction sales are the biggest casualty. Although children's printed book sales are still relatively healthy it cannot be long until the shift to digital occurs in this sector too. In early January 2013 publishers confirmed a huge spike in digital sales over the Christmas period. Children's e-books over Christmas grew at the highest level ever.

The 'standout surprise' in digital sales in 2012 was the proportion of digital sales for YA titles, boosted of course by crossover titles such as *The Hunger Games*. At present more fiction titles are sold as e-books, but non-fiction books still achieve much higher sales in print. At London Book Fair's Digital Minds Conference in April 2012 it was predicted that the 'fast and far-reaching rise in device uptake' means that by 2017 41% of all books sold will be in e-book format and 40% of regular readers will choose e-books. According to the Publishers Association 'the significant growth in the e-book market shows that e-reading is not destined to remain a minority sport… e-book readers are also book buyers… nothing points to the catastrophic cannibalisation of one format by the other, but rather it points to a diversification of the reading audience.' Libraries need to be ready to seize the opportunity e-books represent for growing their customer base.

FLIPS use the attraction and familiarity of the Nintendo DS platform to lure children into some great books. Each cartridge contains several titles from best-selling authors to read onscreen together with additional interactive content like character profiles, mini-games and quizzes to increase the enjoyment of reading as well as secret content which can only be unlocked by collecting special symbols as you read. Using the DS wireless connection allows you to share sample chapters with your friends and unlock more minibooks.

DAISY

DAISY stands for Digital Accessible Information System. It looks like a CD but it is much cleverer. Many books produced for visually impaired people now come in a DAISY format, and the DAISY format is now an internationally recognised format for accessible talking books. The main advantage it gives the reader is in extremely sophisticated bookmarking, so that you can easily search for particular sections, or even particular words. The reader can also insert their own bookmarks. They can be read in three ways – as an audio file with a realistic synthetic voice, as enlarged text on a computer screen or via refreshable Braille. The disadvantage is that they can't be played on an ordinary CD player – you need a special DAISY player or software can be downloaded to enable them to be accessed on a computer. The RNIB is a good source of information about DAISY.

DVD

Film is another way into story for many young people, and it is surprising how many books have been interpreted by film makers over the years. One website which gives a list of such books is Based on the Book (www.mcpl.lib.mo.us/readers/movies/). Films can be particularly useful for students who struggle either with print or the English language – or indeed sensory impairment – by using the increasingly sophisticated subtitling features which often these days include an audio description for visually impaired people as well as the standard subtitling for the hard of hearing.

As part of a recent book week activity one secondary school showed the beginnings of five 'films of books' in the library at lunchtimes over the week, and saw a marked interest in the five titles as a result. The launch of FilmClub (www.filmclub.org) has been used by many school libraries as a way of opening up new avenues for exploring story. Signup is free and screenings are free and the support excellent.

Audio Description

Audio description is a facility which can make all the difference to people with a visual impairment who are trying to enjoy leisure activities alongside sighted people. It provides an extra narration describing the significant visual information – such as body language, facial expression, scenery, action and costumes – that is important for conveying the plot and ambience of a story or event.

As well as films on video and DVD, audio description is available on an increasing range of TV programmes through Freeview or Sky, although not yet on cable. As yet, though, only about 6% of programmes are audio described – about 10 hours a week – and the RNIB is campaigning for this to be increased.

Many contemporary DVDs have audio description within their languages menu and, in addition, the RNIB Home Video service now has 150 audio described film titles available for sale or rental. Quite a few of these are children's and teenage titles.

Book and Author Promotion Websites

The sites chosen for inclusion here are those which add that extra wow factor to the book in some way. There are of course hundreds of others out there and more are being created all the time. They have been included in this Guideline as a way of 'hooking' reluctant readers or non-readers into books through the excitement of games and information all based around books. The sites will be so much better when the participant has read the books concerned – but do not stop them enjoying the site before reading! Many author, publisher and series websites also feature book trailers; teaser video clips designed to hype a book before publication. Such trailers have a particular appeal for those who can read but choose not to. YouTube is another great source of book trailers.

Adam Blade

The Beast Quest books really do come to life on the screen inviting readers to join the tribes in order to join in the quest themselves. As well as the kind of detailed information boys especially love about the different series, defenders and characters the site allows fans to unlock the stunningly illustrated *Book of Beasts*, 'a source of knowledge and secrets about every Beast known to wizard and man in all the lands'. Additional interactive fun stuff includes quizzes, game-playing tournaments, a Beast Name generator, downloads and even a virtual pet to control and prepare for battle! The competitions cleverly refer readers back to the original books inviting them to collect special logos hidden in the stories to win beastly goody-bags. Perfect for existing Beast Quest enthusiasts as well as whetting the appetite of future readers.

http://www.beastquest.co.uk/

Ally Carter

This glossy and glamorous site invites readers to enter the worlds of Carter's two winning series, Gallagher Girls and Heist Academy. Both are laid out in a similar way and offer extracts to download, video trailers and audio extracts expertly read by the author. Background Files contain the usual wallpapers as well as exclusive 'stories behind the stories' classified info and even a Spotify songlist! All very slick and very temptingly packaged.

http://www.gallagheracademy.com/

Angie Sage

A superbly illustrated interactive map forms the basis of this site which invites exploration and ensures engagement. With detailed information about the magykal settings, hidden games and spells, author video interviews and a manuscriptorium introducing all the books in the series, with extracts, there is lots here to extend and enrich the reading experience.

http://www.septimusheap.com/

Anne Fine

This is an interesting and accessible author website with all the usual ingredients – biography, list of books, frequently asked questions, news etc.

A gem is found in the section 'Children's Laureate'. When Anne Fine was the Children's Laureate between 2001-2003, she headed a project called 'My Home Library' which aimed to put books in children's homes, to encourage them to have books around them all the time and to value books as precious possessions. There is a link from the Children's Laureate page to the 'zippy site' (www.myhomelibrary.org) which is a celebration of the joy of owning books of your own. The focus of the site is a collection of beautifully designed book plates (you can also find a set of e-bookplates by clicking on the link on the Anne Fine homepage, which can be personalised in a similar way to an e-greetings card), but there is also a review section, which is divided into reviews by the author and reviews by young readers, and a fascinating history of the practice of using book plates. There is also a section on finding second hand books and starting your own home collection, and a link to the part of the project which aimed to put books into the hands of visually impaired students. The Home Library project not only donated books from Clearvision (www.clearvisionproject.org) to Braille-reading children, they produced special bookmarks for this often-neglected group as well. Clearvision books have clear Braille pages interleaved with regular print, so that a sighted person can share a book with a blind child, and they operate a postal lending service so that school librarians can borrow their books on behalf of their students.

The Home Library link turns this fairly ordinary author website into a very powerful advocate of the power and value of books, and the pleasures of owning books of your own.

www.annefine.co.uk

Benjamin Zephaniah

Benjamin Zephaniah's website is fascinating and unique. It's not the conventional professionally designed website, but it manages to be accessible and easy to navigate while having a strong flavour of the personality of this most passionate and articulate of men. It would appeal to students who are excited by words and ideas – and students who are thoughtful without yet being switched on to reading. There is lots on this website about Benjamin Zephaniah's political beliefs – the section on why he refused an OBE is particularly interesting and would provide a good basis for discussion, for instance, but there are plenty of examples of his poetry and other entertaining sections as well.

One of the sections is specifically for children. He gives a biography and an account of some of his books for children, together with links including some to reviews of his work by children. In fact, the practice which is followed throughout the site of putting the links at the relevant place in the text of the website is easier to follow than a separate links page. At the bottom of the Kidz page are articles and interviews as well as snippets of some of his books. The section for teens is similarly structured. Benjamin Zephaniah is primarily an oral poet and as well as plenty of examples of his poetry on the site there is a link to the One Little Indian website (www.onelittleshop.com) where users can listen to snippets of his latest work.

www.benjaminzephaniah.com

Cathy Cassidy

Every bit as colourful as the characters in her stories the Cathy Cassidy website is a brilliant way to engage reluctant girls and hook them into reading. As well as the usual author, book and series info this rainbow site offers girls a space to show off their own pictures, drawings and writing as well as a writing workshop full of tips and ideas. Fab Freebies and Kool Downloads include everything you need to organise your own Friendship Festival, easy-to-follow cake recipes and exciting craft activities as well as a chance to sign up to a Friendship Charter and receive certificates for being a great mate. On a more serious note, Cathy draws on her own experience as an agony aunt addressing some common problems for her readership in her usual matter-of-fact, light-hearted tone.

www.cathycassidy.com

Charlie Higson

Higson's zombie book series is brought terrifyingly to life in this slick site offering extracts, video trailers, zombie downloads and a hilarious 'zombie me' image generator. Boys will be powerless to resist!

www.the-enemy.co.uk

Chris Priestley

A brilliantly conceived website with a super scary soundtrack. The interactive animation for the first book, *Uncle Montague's Tales of Terror*, is particularly addictive, while there is plenty of illustrated information available about the other books, all with downloadable extracts.

www.talesofterror.co.uk

Darren Shan

This is a very comprehensive website all written by the author himself. It is fascinating both about the author personally and about his literary creations, the vampires and the demons. It is imaginatively designed with lots of extras such as downloads of wallpaper and screensavers, and a long and chatty blog. It could well appeal to reluctant readers – in fact if students first encounter Darren Shan through the website, they will most likely come and pester the librarian for his books as well!

Darren Shan, real name Darren O'Shaughnessy, is a young Irish writer who found popularity with his first children's book, *Cirque du Freak*. This turned out to be the first in a series of twelve books called 'The Saga of Darren Shan' which found huge popularity in many countries. The rest, as they say, is history, but Darren Shan, far from retreating into some kind of ivory tower is as accessible as possible for a major author. He has created a website which is entertaining, detailed and personal, yet easy to read and accessible. The downloads do not interfere with the content of the site, which will satisfy the curiosity of the most ardent of fans. It includes detailed summaries with commentary by the author of all of his books, lots of reviews and cover illustrations. There is also the usual biography, photos and audio files of many interviews, plus a monthly update of what Darren Shan has been up to and a gallery of fan art as well as a brilliantly informative creative writing section packed full of advice on writing your own stories.

The website is interactive with links to a message board (note of caution: it's not clear to what extent this is moderated) and includes many contributions from young fans, and Darren positively welcomes and promises to reply to letters. He also welcomes enquiries about school visits. Altogether a good website to recommend to a gothic-minded student.

www.darrenshan.com

Derek Landy

One of those exciting sites which really brings the world of the author and his novels to life. As well as video author interviews and story summaries, each with a downloadable extract, there are copious character notes and a huge Fun and Games section. With MP3s and spooky Skulduggery ringtones, screensavers, wallpapers, avatar widgets, online gameplay, competitions, scary personalised videos to send to your friends and a chance to sign up for the Munchkin Army, everyone will want to turn to the books after this!

http://www.skulduggerypleasant.co.uk/

Gillian Cross

A straightforward and accessible website which apart from anything else will absorb the reader who says 'I have read *The Demon Headmaster*, what can I read now?' It hasn't got a lot of flashy animations or downloads, but this means that those students who find some websites just too complicated and confusing to navigate because of fussy screens, sounds, animations and suchlike, will perhaps be able to use it more independently than some of the others reviewed here. The text is a clear light coloured font on a dark blue background. This is an ideal combination for many children with impaired vision, and has also been shown to be helpful for children with specific learning difficulties such as dyslexia.

The different parts of the site are listed in a menu down the right hand side and include a biography, some frequently asked questions and a very comprehensive list of Gillian Cross's books. One interesting feature is a list of text messaging symbols (maybe more helpful for adults!) which includes some which will only be found in *Beware of the Demon Headmaster*. This might inspire some young people to invent their own.

The text is written in Gillian Cross's friendly and clear style, and the author encourages readers to send in their queries or comments. The website is something of a portal, as there is also a good page of links which would encourage the student to take their enquiries further, whether they want to find out more about Gillian Cross herself or children's books generally.

www.gillian-cross.co.uk

Jacqueline Wilson

Tweenage girls will spend hours on this site while dipping in and out of the books and finding new titles to try. An interactive bookshelf organises Wilson's novels by theme (love, friendship, family, issues and humour), then lets you see inside the book, rate and review each title and watch short book trailer ads. There's lots of easily accessible information about the author, illustrator and characters, competitions and links to other interesting book-related websites, all presented in the lively, colourful style you'd expect. If that wasn't enough there's Fun and Games to be had in the form of online doodling, downloadable puzzles, jokes, quizzes, polls, e-cards and even a chance to see your own face on the cover of a Jacqueline Wilson novel.

http://www.jacquelinewilson.co.uk/

Louise Rennison

Rennison's fabby website is everything you'd expect from the Teen of Queen and is full of opportunities for girls to get involved, whether it's signing up to the Ace Gang with its Fab Forum or posting photos in the Friends Gallery. With a range of video trailers for the books, extracts (including audio) and interviews with Rennison herself, it's a very friendly site with plenty of competitions, prizes and treats on offer as well as the facility for 'little chumettes' to ask questions of the author.

http://www.georgia-nicolson.co.uk/

Marcus Sedgwick

The six books in the Raven Mysteries series are brought brilliantly to life in this stunning site with its spooky audio soundtrack. There's a chance to Meet the Family in a fact-filled portrait gallery and Take a Tour of Otherland Castle through an interactive map.

You can download pdfs of the first chapters of each book and listen to samples of the audio versions. Those signed up to the Goth-Froth club also access sneaky peeks of the next book. Registered Goth-Frothers can also play games, download screensavers, enter competitions and sign up for the newsletter. This is not a huge site but it is incredibly well-designed and meets readers at just the right level.

http://www.ravenmysteries.co.uk/

Mark Walden

Designed to look like an official government agency site, the Hivehub hides information about the books (with downloadable pdf extracts) and inside author info and interviews. Boys in particular will enjoy the online Grapple Training, while Streams Training will determine which of the four streams readers belong to, making them part of the book action. And because every evil super-villain needs an evil laugh there's even an evil laugh generator with mixer track, speed control and the option to send it to a friend!

www.hivehub.co.uk

Michael Grant

With cinema-quality book trailers, MP3 author interviews, downloadable wallpapers, icons and chapter samplers this is an effective and very visual taster of the novels for those, boys particularly, who can read but tend not to.

http://www.egmont.co.uk/gone/

Morris Gleitzman

A bright and breezy website with lots to explore. Morris Gleitzman's website is written in his usual chatty, humorous style with lots of links. The site is updated regularly and is pretty accessible – you can navigate it using just keystrokes if you're not a mouse user – and there are tips on making the site more accessible in a quick link from the homepage. The text is clear and the background uncluttered, although pictures throughout make the site friendly and warm looking.

As well as being entertaining and humorous this website would be really good for someone who had to 'do a project' on Morris Gleitzman as there is lots of autobiographical information both as a list of dates and some funny stories, together with pictures and even his school reports! There is a big section of 'MAQs' – Morris's Most Asked Questions – and loads of stuff about all his books, including audio and video excerpts with text to read along to. The Bookshelf page has all Morris's books on it. Clicking on the book brings up information about the story and another link leads to a chapter online with an audio file as well. Parts of the site talk about the writing process and users are also encouraged to write to Morris directly. This page includes some practical and sensitive guidance to children on sending emails safely.

All in all, this is a website which might well send a child from the computer to try one of Morris's books in print, or audio. The point is made throughout the site that many of the books are available in audio – and if a student is tempted away from the PC to try something new, that can only be a good thing.

www.morrisgleitzman.com

P. C. Cast

This is a huge site with excerpts and video trailers for each book and novella as well as heaps of background information including a tour of the setting, and essentials such as interactive rune charts, rituals and spells. Real fans can design their own vampyre tattoo and read the online Year Book as well as read extracts from the graphic novel versions.

http://www.houseofnightseries.com/

Pottermore

The much-hyped and long-awaited Pottermore site aims to 'build an exciting online experience around the Harry Potter books', opening up the original novels in a whole new way as well as revealing exclusive new writing from J. K. Rowling. The site allows users to try on the sorting hat, overcome magical challenges, compete for the house cup and go on the Pottermore journey with their friends. This is a text-lite, visually stunning site which could well form a useful bridge from the films to the novels for those with less reading stamina.

http://www.pottermore.com/

Quentin Blake

This would be a good website to send someone to if they like drawing and art but aren't yet hooked into books. Blake's books are mainly aimed at younger children and it's true that the downloads are for children at primary school, but his work appeals to people of all ages. It is a fairly small and straightforward website – it hasn't got lots of animations etc so will load and run easily and efficiently, and is easy to navigate. The site is illustrated throughout with Blake's pictures and there is a section about Blake's books, his life and his relationship with authors, especially Roald Dahl, a section for children packed full of activities and downloads and also a section for teachers about using Blake's picture books in the classroom.

Blake writes in an easy chatty style about his illustrations and this site would inform and entertain a student who enjoys Blake's work, perhaps sending them back to the books with something new to look for and an added dimension to discover.

www.quentinblake.com

Roald Dahl

This is a hugely entertaining and sophisticated website. Probably not one for people struggling with screen readers or with limited bandwidth, those who are able to access it will nonetheless be engrossed and captivated. Roald Dahl is one of the few authors that even non-readers can name, and this group together with those who are already fans of his books would be likely to get the most out of this site. Young people who loved Roald Dahl's books in primary school but have since lost the reading habit may well be tempted back into the world of books by this site.

The menu page is clear and interesting leading to lots of games, animations, e-cards, quizzes and funny noises as well as plenty of useful information for the Roald Dahl fan as well as the young researcher. There are also features for teachers, and some pages for which you have to join the Roald Dahl Club – any under-thirteens can join, free, by filling in a simple online form.

www.roalddahl.com

Robert Muchamore

Muchamore's site hides a wealth of content designed to lure boys into books, and many girls too would find much to enjoy here. Author facts, writing tips, book information are all here but so too is a free downloadable, never before published, first draft novel, *Home* (not suitable for younger readers). The dedicated *Henderson Boys* site is more interactive with sample chapters downloadable as pdfs or webpages, maps, games and wallpaper. The *Cherub Campus* site is even more sophisticated with the same sample chapters, background facts and character profiles but also lots of Bonus Stories and a link to Muchamore's dedicated YouTube channel and fan forums.

www.muchamore.com

Suzanne Collins

This is a slick and stylish introduction to the books, the author and the blockbuster film which uses a series of thrilling book trailers, video author interviews, MP3 readings by the author and sample chapter downloads to really bring the stories to life. Clever simulations allow fans to test their own skills and abilities and determine their chances of survival in a situation like *The Hunger Games*. Anyone hungry for more will enjoy the suggestions of similar novels to try with links to their social media sites for more information.

http://www.thehungergames.co.uk/

Terry Deary

Although plans for a Horrible History virtual world have now been shelved, the HH website contains much to lead readers to explore the books. Interactive games take the same irreverent tone as the books, there's also fun stuff to download, printables, wallpapers, competitions, character profiles, news and much more.

http://horrible-histories.co.uk/

Will Hill

With its hi-tech, hi-risk feel this is another superb site for hooking thrillseekers into books. Alongside the author information, book summaries, wallpaper and text alert tone downloads are gripping video evidence and an intriguing weapons archive. Extra content such as family trees and authorisation codes all pull the reader into the action, and into the books.

http://www.department19exists.com/

Reading Promotion Websites

Bringing books to life — a selected A-Z

The sites chosen for inclusion here are those which all bring books and writing to life in some way or offer ways of interacting with writers and other readers which might just spark an interest in those who struggle with reading for whatever reason. They are of course, just the tip of the iceberg!

Behind the Bookshelf

Behind the Bookshelf is a brilliant new resource for bringing books off the shelf, leading readers to new books and authors and for demystifying the writing process. It consists of a library of short video clips of authors reading aloud from their own work and also talking about different parts of the process from finding the right narrative voice to creating characters and what to do when you get stuck. Top notch authors featured include Darren Shan and David Almond, Sophie McKenzie, Melvin Burgess, Malorie Blackman, Marcus Sedgwick and Morris Gleitzman. Librarians and teachers can customise the site and create their own libraries and lesson plans.

Behind the Bookshelf is the next best thing to having an author visit your library and will inspire just as much enthusiasm for reading and writing. Sign up for a free trial.

http://www.behindthebookshelf.co.uk/

Bookwink

Bookwink's mission is 'to inspire kids to read'. It aims to connect kids to books that will make them excited about reading through podcasting and video. What this has produced, in effect, is a collection of 3 minute video booktalks, all archived, and a large database of exciting books searchable by subject, author, title or grade level (since the site is American, age 9-14). Additional 'readalikes' are also given and a themed podcast is available. It is constantly being updated. Follow Bookwink on twitter @Bookwink.

www.bookwink.com

Channel 4 BookBox

Although quite an old site now, BookBox aims to put young readers 'in touch with their favourite authors and their books'. This is achieved through a series of engaging video clips and podcasts with over 30 authors, poets and illustrators popular at KS2 and KS3.

Separate sections include Secret Passages – suggestions for those stuck for something to read with clear extracts to aid choice, a Writer's Toolkit answering those tricky questions which trouble aspiring young authors from how do I begin my stories and how do I know when to stop, to how should my characters speak and how can I find interesting words? Finally the games section, though simple, contains lots of fun and exceptionally easy to navigate options from fridge magnet poetry to limericks, many of which can be printed for display.

http://www.channel4learning.com/sites/bookbox/home.htm

Figment

Figment is intended to 'encourage the reading habits of a generation' through 'sharing writing, connecting with other readers and discovering new stories and authors'. Books and writing are organised into genres and lots of tips for improving your own writing are given together with competitions, many linked to published books. Figment also offers the chance to read excerpts and engage with authors online as well as take part in the reading/writing-linked forums and groups.

Established in 2010 by the AASL, Figment also promotes itself as a powerful learning tool and advice is available for educators to help use the site to its full advantage with teenagers. Follow @figmentfiction on twitter or on Facebook.

http://figment.com

Guardian Children's Books

The revamped Guardian Children's Book site is 'all about children', written by children for children; although the title children is a bit of a misnomer as there is lots on offer here for discerning teens too. Most importantly this is 'their space' to find out about, review and discuss books in all their formats. With its clear, attractive layout, free extracts and interactivity there is plenty here to tempt everyone into reading. A regular podcast feature offers extracts from books read by the author and an interview feature with questions from readers. 'Trailblazer' video extracts and author interviews are also usefully included together with brilliant features such as best first lines, 'how to draw' tutorials by leading picture book illustrators and plenty of themed quizzes. Julia Eccleshare's 'Book Doctor' column will provide food for thought for librarians, teachers and parents while children are invited to sign up and submit their own reviews and features and take part in regular online discussion groups. Follow new content on twitter @GdnChildrensBks and @GuardianTeenBks.

http://www.guardian.co.uk/childrens-books-site

Love Reading

Love Reading exists to 'help you choose your next book'. Set up initially as an independent bookselling site for adults with 'like-for-like recommendations, there is now a New Gen section useful for recommending to older teens who can download extracts of the featured books, create wishlists and use the Love Reading Facebook app to share their reading with friends: adding their favourite authors and books to their Facebook profile and getting updates on the latest books in their favourite genres.

The Audiobooks on CD section offers informative reviews and monthly listings of new audio releases for adults and children as well as themed podcasts. A clearly signposted e-books section features monthly recommended reads in a wide variety of formats.

It is worth noting that the formats in which each book entry on Love Reading is available is very clearly marked. It is easy to see at a glance whether the book is available in print, audio CD, iBook, ePub, Google e-books, Kobo or Kindle format and purchasing/downloading is very simple.

Follow Love Reading on twitter: @lovereadinguk

www.lovereading.co.uk

LoveReading4Kids

The children's version of the site, LoveReading4Kids, has been 'created to be the ultimate children's online, independent bookstore' and is every bit as user-friendly and accessible as its adult relation.

The e-books section highlights an e-book of the month as well as featuring a monthly round up of new and recommended e-books, each with an extract to try before you buy. Audiobooks are also available for purchase on CD or as a download. Age guidance is offered on all books featured on LoveReading4Kids.

http://www.lovereading4kids.co.uk/genre/ebk/Ebooks.html

Movellas

Movellas is an online community which allows you to read, write and share stories and gain feedback from other readers. The 2013 World Book Day YA app is powered by Movellas and gives young people the opportunity to choose which submitted stories they want to see featured on the app alongside those by established, published authors like Chris Ryan and Dawn O'Porter. Stories on the site are clearly organised into genres and a variety of groups open up debate around stories.

Movellas also supports the Young Movellist of the Year award. The opportunities for interaction offered by sites such as Movellas will prove attractive to teenagers. Follow Movellas on twitter: @movellas

http://www.movellas.com/

National Nonfiction Day

The NNFD site is a wealth of information about all things non-fiction. Although it promotes a very important day in the reading calendar it provides brilliant reading suggestions around themes such as Creatures, Machines, People, the Earth, the past, the Universe and Your Life with lots of downloadable activity sheets and sample pages from featured books. A colourful week-by-week calendar offers fascinating facts and talking points on a huge range of topics and is bound to lead young readers to want to find out more.

www.nnfd.org

Reading Matters

This is a book recommendation website run by Jill Marshall. Although the number of books reviewed on the site is relatively small, they are of high quality books and well worth browsing through.

There are 328 reviews (accessed April 2012) which are easy to search by title, author or genre. The different genres are presented as booklists in a broad range of subjects and one highly attractive feature of the site is a bookchooser where, using the interactive bookfinder form, the user has to say how important various features are in a book, for instance adventure, romance, humour etc. A list of books is then presented, together with reviews. Another section gives a short list of articles about books discussing particular questions. One interesting example is 'Power tends to corrupt'. Readers are also encouraged to add their own opinions of the books reviewed and there are contributions from children all over the world.

This would be a good website for a teenager to browse through. It's accessible using speech synthesis software and its simple yet effective layout is visually clear and easy to read. I would use this site for several groups of pupils – the bright ones who are in danger of being turned off to reading, as this website may well lead them on to find new authors and a forum to interact with other teenagers – and the ones who find it hard to settle down to read but would benefit from half an hour finding out about some good quality reads. It's also perfectly suitable for able students with physical or sensory impairment who enjoy reading about books.

www.readingmatters.co.uk

ReadingZone

ReadingZone is a huge site containing 'everything you need to know about children's books and authors' with dedicated 'zones' for families, schools, libraries, children and young adults. Positively bursting with book news, reviews, author interviews, excerpts, competitions and games, you'll wonder how you ever managed without it!

Children's Zone is completely child-friendly – review books online, complete interactive wordsearches, design your own bookmarks, find reading and what next? suggestions.

Young Adult Zone has a far darker more sophisticated feel with bookbites of book news but lots of goody giveaways and a chance to post your own reviews and a message board for discussing reading.

The School and Library Zones offer reading lists, ideas, initiatives and resources galore, discussion forums and downloadable extracts from new and upcoming titles.

FamilyZone offers useful age specific tips for encouraging reading and suggests titles suitable for each group as well as the facility to create your own lists of books to explore further.

Although 'books in alternative formats' are not explicit on the site there is much here to hook everyone into reading whatever their feelings towards it and the huge enthusiasm with which it is compiled is irresistible.

Follow @readingzone on twitter for news and updates.

www.readingzone.com

Readplus

Readplus is a collection of over 10,000 books and films for 5–18s organised by theme. As well as countless reviews there are lots of links to teacher resources and reading group guides as well as the facility to create your own 'Who else writes like?' posters and bookmarks. Although the site is Australian in origin there is plenty for use worldwide. This outstanding digital resource is available on subscription only with a site licence. Details on the website. UK schools can subscribe via Carel Press with a site licence and there is a free trial option.

Follow Readplus on twitter @readplus

www.readplus.com.au

http://www.carelpress.co.uk/eresources/readplus/index.html

Spinebreakers

Spinebreakers, according to their website, are 'story-surfing, web-exploring, word-loving, day-dreaming, reader/writer, artist/thinkers aged 13–18'. The site itself is 'where the world inside a book can come to life' and contains reviews (including films) and author interviews (including videoclips), audio extracts, alternate endings and illustrations, copious competitions and topical forums, short stories and poems – all written by teenage 'crew' contributors. With its clear, sophisticated, teen-friendly layout and highly visual content this is one site guaranteed to draw readers in – and most importantly, keep them coming back. This is the perfect way to get creative with books.

Spinebreakers is also on Facebook http://www.facebook.com/spinebreakers and provides regular updates on twitter @Spinebreakers.

www.spinebreakers.co.uk

Stories from the Web

This website, hosted by Birmingham Libraries, won 'The UK e-well being award' in 2004. It's a massive celebration of books, and reading and encourages students to interact with the site by sending in their own writing, illustrations and reviews, play games and enter competitions. There are three sections, one for pre-school children, one for ages 7–11 and one for 11–14 each with its own age-appropriate feel and set-up. It's well worth looking at, both as a source of support for reader development activities at many levels, and for encouraging students themselves to explore. It's bright and attractive with lots of different features to attract everyone, and with straightforward language and clear fonts, it would be accessible to most students as well, including those with extra challenges. It would mainly appeal to students at the younger end of the secondary age range and is attractive and jazzy enough to tempt those who are beginning to reject libraries and books as staid and old-fashioned.

This is a highly recommended website. Its infectious enthusiasm for everything to do with books will stimulate and engross the young people who explore it and its huge range of things to read and do will foster and nurture any kernel of interest in reading within them.

Although the site originally offered access through subscribing public library authorities it is now available on a subscription basis to schools with the aim of developing readers and inspiring writers in a safe online environment. The pricing structure for primary schools is now available and the secondary schools offer will be available soon (www.storiesfromthewebschools.org/). A trial is possible.

www.storiesfromtheweb.org

World Book Day

As well as information about WBD, the website contains hundreds of printable activities and interactive resources to bring books to life for nursery, primary and secondary schools as well as libraries. There are book-themed games, video book trailers and webcasts of the Biggest Book Show on Earth starring some amazing authors and illustrators.

The Storytime Online section allows you to watch an array of stars reading children's books and stories, all clearly arranged by target age group while Storycraft features video clips of 'amazing authors giving top tips on creating your own brilliant stories'.

The free Books Alive augmented reality app for iOS and Android brings the covers of the WBD books to life with exclusive animations, while the Movellas WBD YA app features new short stories by top authors including Patrick Ness and Dave Cousins. The WBD website aims to become the go-to site for all things books throughout the year not just for World Book Day. With its chatty style, attractive presentation and imaginative ideas, WBD is a great resource for all kinds of reading for all kinds of readers.

Follow WBD on twitter @WorldBookDayUK

http://www.worldbookday.com/

http://www.worldbookday.com/storycraft/

A directory of leading suppliers

The normal copyright and licensing regulations apply to digital and audio resources. Not all of the sites below allow library lending or learning platform hosting and readers should check subscription details carefully. As more young people access these types of resources on their own devices though, some of these websites are well worth recommending to students.

Audible

Digital books available for download from the UK's largest provider.

By either paying a subscription or purchasing individual titles, audio books can be downloaded from the audible.co.uk website. There are literally thousands of titles to choose from in many different genres.

Books from Audible can be read in three different ways – by downloading to a portable device or burning onto a CD; streaming audio onto a computer while it is connected to the Internet; or by downloading and listening using iTunes, Windows Media Player or Audible Manager, which is freely downloadable from the website. The website also indicates which devices are compatible with the available formats and although all this seems complicated the process is actually quite straightforward and all the information you need is easily located within the website.

The audio books in the section for children and young adults are generally mainstream, popular titles. Their attraction for those young people who are becoming reluctant to read is the format which enables them to be read on MP3 players or other portable devices – so nobody need know you are listening to a story instead of music.

www.audible.co.uk

> Audible Ltd, Colet Court, 100 Hammersmith Road, London, W6 7JP
> customercare@audible.co.uk or 0800 496 2455

Audiogo

Audiogo (previously known as BBC Audio) offers large print books, audio books and playaways for libraries, with showrooms in Bath and Preston. An increasing number of titles are available for lending through digital platforms. A variety of customisable Monthly Standing Order plans are available to libraries for new and popular titles in all formats. See their catalogues for details.

http://www.audiogo.co.uk/

www.bbcaudiobooks.com/libraries/

http://www.bbcaudiobooks.com/libraries/ViewCatalogues.aspx

> St James House, The Square, Lower Bristol Road, Bath BA2 3BH
> info@audiogo.co.uk or 01225 443400

Badger Learning

The popular Badger Learning reading books aimed at engaging reluctant and struggling readers are now available for digital download. Each title in the series has between 1,000 and 2,000 words, a reading age of 7.5 to 8 years and an interest level of 8 to 14 years. Titles can be downloaded individually or site licences are available.

Series currently available in print and digital format include *Alien Detective Agency*, *Full Flight Heroes and Heroines*, *Full Flight Gripping Stories* and *Full Flight Adventure*.

http://www.badgerlearning.co.uk/promotions/ebooks/

Barrington Stoke

Barrington Stoke specialises in fiction and resources for reluctant, dyslexic, disenchanted and under-confident readers. CDs also available for some titles.

www.barringtonstoke.co.uk

Barrington Stoke, 18 Walker Street, Edinburgh, EH3 7L
Tel: 0131 225 4113

BMW Audiobooks

Most free downloadable audio books are titles which are out of copyright and therefore classic (old) books, short stories, poetry and plays. However, the BMW series of short stories are absolutely up to date and as all the reader has to do is register on the site, they are really easy to access.

A major character in each story is a BMW car, but the stories are much more than just an extended advertisement for BMW! They can either be opened directly to play in Windows Media Player or equivalent, or saved to an MP3 player to be listened to on the move. They are all adult stories, but would appeal to older secondary age students.

http://audio-books-for-everyone.com/bmw-audio-books.html

Books Should Be Free

Books Should Be Free has thousands of free audiobooks in MP3, iTunes or iPod format. Arranged by genre with a children's section.

http://www.booksshouldbefree.com/

Calibre Audio Library

Calibre is a registered charity which now supplies audio books free of charge to over 20,000 people who can't use standard print books. This might be people with a visual impairment – although you don't have to be registered blind or partially sighted to join – or it could be people who can't physically hold a book, for instance or those with dyslexia who find accessing standard texts problematic and demotivating. Calibre has traditionally been a cassette library but now operates a digital service and borrowers can obtain audio books on MP3 discs as well. One of the charity's main guiding principles is to produce books in formats which people can use on ordinary mainstream equipment, and so no special player is needed for Calibre books – cassettes can be played on Walkmans or traditional cassette players, and MP3 discs can be played, as well as on MP3 players, on computers, some modern CD players and in DVD players as well. You can also download to an iPod or similar player. They will also work on the specialist DAISY players (see elsewhere in this publication for information on DAISY).

The audio books in the catalogue are all unabridged and recorded by volunteer voice professionals. They are of extremely high standard. Although most of their catalogue of 8,000 titles is aimed at an adult audience, Calibre do have over 1,400 children's leisure reading titles, and young people are allowed to borrow from the adult list as long as it's not an x-rated book. About 360 titles are added each year – almost one a day – and the new digital service will help text-impaired young people to access books in a way which fits in with their lifestyle.

The dedicated Young Calibre website (http://www.youngcalibre.org.uk/) is very engaging and user-friendly, allowing customisation to enhance readability whatever the reading impairment. As well as themed booklists the site also offers young people the possibility of building their own booklists online.

This is a very useful website to know about – either to recommend to the individual student or for the librarian to use to help the student choose titles, perhaps for someone who hasn't read anything for a while because of their disability. A school library can open a group membership and hold up to eight titles at one time which can be changed as often as necessary for a small annual subscription (£50 at the time of writing). Books are exchanged by post, using the 'Articles for the Blind' scheme, which means that no charge is made for postage.

http://www.youngcalibre.org.uk/

Calibre Audio Library, Aylesbury, Bucks HP22 5XQ
enquiries@calibre.org.uk or 01296 432339

Classical Comics

Classical Comics is a UK publisher creating graphic novel versions of classical literature in original, plain and quick text formats.

http://www.classicalcomics.com/

> Classical Comics Limited, PO Box 7280, Litchborough, Towcester, NN12 9AR
>
> info@classicalcomics.com or 0845 812 3000

ClearVision

ClearVision is a UK postal lending library for dual Braille/print, Moon/print and tactile books for children which makes them ideal for sharing. While the majority of books are mainstream titles for those learning to read or the newly fluent there is also an expanding collection of books on popular National Curriculum topics and books for teenagers with low reading ages.

http://www.clearvisionproject.org/

> ClearVision, 61 Princes Way, London, SW19 6JB
>
> info@clearvisionproject.org or 020 8789 9575

Graphic Shakespeare

Graphic Shakespeare offers full folio, full colour graphic novel versions of Shakespeare's most popular plays.

http://www.graphicshakespeare.com/

> Can of Worms Enterprises Ltd, 8 Peacock Yard, Iliffe Street, London, SE17 3LH
>
> info@canofwormspress.co.uk or 020 7708 2942

International Children's Digital Library

ICDL is an extensive site which aims to make 'the best of children's literature worldwide available online free of charge'. Search the downloadable content by language, book length, genre, interest age, even book cover colour.

http://en.childrenslibrary.org/

i-Stars

The i-Stars website provides e-books for school and home. It contains over 100 e-books from a range of publishers in a range of formats with various licencing options for use on the whiteboard, on a PC or on mobile devices. The site is easily navigable and particularly good for finding books for struggling or resistant readers from KS1 to upper KS3. It brings together popular series such as *Magic Mates, Mystery Mob, Shades, Downloads,*

Dangerous Games, The Extraordinary Files, Superscripts, Shadows and *Graphic Universe*. Extensive guidance on content, reading age and interest level is given for each title featured. Some titles have audio. Students can also review titles they have enjoyed or upload e-books they have created. The site also offers useful advice and ideas on using e-books in the classroom or library.

http://istars.education.co.uk/

JCS Online Resources for Schools

JCS provide negotiated price access to a range of online subscription resources for use across the curriculum and for reference.

http://www.jcsonlineresources.org/

Large Print Bookshop

The Large Print Bookshop is the UK's largest stockist of large print books with over 20,000 fiction and nonfiction titles produced in 16 point type. While the majority of titles are aimed at adults they would be suitable for older teenagers. Some children's books are also included.

www.largeprintbookshop.co.uk

6 The Quadrant, Newark Close, Royston , Herts. SG8 5HL
01763 255 022

Librivox

Librivox is an online collection of freely downloadable audio books. The titles are all in the public domain and therefore free from restrictions on copying, lending and sharing. The website is American and relies on volunteers to record the books. Despite this the quality is reasonable and is a good way of making books accessible to a range of students who aren't able to read books from the library in a traditional way. The website started in August 2005 and has grown steadily ever since. Librivox's aim is to 'liberate' all works in the public domain.

Clicking on a title brings up a range of options – you can access the e-text of the book or the Wikipedia entry; and a choice of methods of downloading the work. Therefore the reader can either read the text on a screen, download it to an MP3 player, or listen to it directly from a desktop or laptop computer. This brings benefits for two specific groups of young people – those who have difficulties with text because of poor vision or some physical impairment which means that they can't hold a book properly, and those who have been 'turned off' traditional library use for whatever reason but still enjoy a story and are comfortable with today's electronic media.

www.librivox.org

Listening Books

Listening Books provides a postal and internet-based audiobook library service for anyone who finds it difficult to read in the usual way. Books can be posted out on CD or accessed via Downloadable, an audio download service, to PC or portable device with titles available for adults and children.

http://www.listening-books.org.uk/

Listening Books, 12 Lant Street, London, SE1 1QH
info@listening-books.org.uk or 020 7407 9417

Living Paintings Trust

The Living Paintings Trust is a specialist charity which aims to bring pictures to life for blind and partially sighted children, young people and adults. It works through families, carers and schools as well as with individuals in order to maximise the opportunities for visually impaired people to experience art. The loans are free and, as they use the 'Articles for the Blind' postal scheme, there is no charge for postage and packing either.

This is a really useful charity to know about if there are students with poor vision in a school; there are so many activities which disabled students are excluded from and this is one service that the library could offer to give children a new experience and a new way of 'reading'.

The Trust send out packs with three components: a raised image, known as a thermoform, which explains the shape of the picture and other special characteristics; an audio description which tells the story of the picture and provides instructions for touching and interpreting the thermoform, and a colour reproduction of the picture which make it possible for it to be shared with sighted people.

The packs are divided into various age ranges. The introductory pack for secondary age children, for instance, contains 11 tactile pictures and 5 cassette tapes covering things such as body language, facial expressions, building a landscape etc. Some of the packs cover curriculum areas such as Kings and Queens, Art in Science and People in Paintings. As well as the thermoforms which guide the touch reader through the picture, the cassettes give background to the painter and the period in which the painting was created. There is also a whole series of familiar picture books such as *The Very Hungry Caterpillar*, which might come in handy if a whole class is looking at picture books, and packs exploring the books of Roald Dahl.

www.livingpaintings.org   @livingPaintings

Magic Town

Magic Town is a virtual world for picture books aimed at children from 2 to 6 years old and encourages parents to share stories with their children. It includes well-known, well-loved characters such as *Elmer* and *Winnie the Witch* produced by a variety of mainstream publishers like OUP, Hachette, Egmont, Usborne and Little Tiger. Magic Town is divided into different character 'houses' each including animations, games, videos and stories (read aloud) as well as e-books. Some content is free with a monthly subscription available to unlock extra titles. 10 to 15 new stories are added to the platform monthly. Future developments include an iPad version, an e-commerce site and a free schools version.

http://www.magictown.com/

National Blind Children's Society

Provides customised large print books for children and teenagers with sight problems.

www.nbcs.org.uk

Bradbury House, Market Street, Highbridge, Somerset TA9 3BW
enquiries@nbcs.org.uk or 01278 764764

Information about their CustomEyes book service (covering fact, popular fiction, revision guides and children's classics for home and school, tailormade in both font-size and format to suit individual children's needs) is available.

http://nbcs.org.uk/customeyes

National Talking Newspapers and Magazines

NTNM is part of RNIB and provides all national, daily and Sunday newspapers in accessible formats including audio, CD, DAISY and electronic download for an annual subscription per title. A number of magazines are also available which will be of interest to older teenagers.

http://www.tnauk.org.uk/

National Talking Newspapers and Magazines, National Recording Centre,. Heathfield, East Sussex, TN21 8DB
info@tnauk.org.uk or 01435 866102

Oxford Owls

Oxford Owls is a free, easily navigable website designed to support reading at primary level. As well as help and advice for parents the site offers a huge variety of free e-books, many with audio. Books are clearly divided into age categories and include titles from Oxford Reading Tree and Project X. Advice includes up to date reading lists from expert, Nikki Gamble, which will appeal to students of all reading abilities well into KS3. Those working with struggling readers in lower secondary as well as primary will find this site invaluable.

http://www.oxfordowl.co.uk/reading

Penguin Podcast and Penguin e-books

For older students on the move this is a fortnightly regular podcast of news, extracts, features and author interviews from the publisher. Be warned – this is aimed at an adult audience and content may be unsuitable for younger readers. What is effectively a short radio programme (about 18 to 20 minutes) can be listened to directly from a computer or downloaded onto an MP3 player. It would perhaps be useful for an older student who enjoys stories and still has an interest in books but is in danger of losing the reading habit because their lifestyle is too busy. It keeps the listener up to date with news of new books via iTunes or an RSS feed and provides quite long extracts.

Penguin also has a substantial and rapidly growing collection of e-books, all produced in .epub format. As yet, these are not suitable for the library as they can only be accessed on the computer from which they were bought. They have to be paid for directly using a credit or debit card but are much cheaper than the paperback version of the same title. It's worth knowing about as you might recommend them to this group of older students to help them to keep up with the reading habit no matter where they are. E-books can be downloaded onto a computer or a hand held computer device and they use software such as Adobe Acrobat, Microsoft Reader or Palm Reader. There is also a text-to-audio facility on the Adobe Acrobat version, and in the sample chapters provided in the Microsoft Reader format, enabling these to be accessed by visually impaired people who use speech synthesisers on their computers. This would be a synthetic voice rather than an actor but synthetic voices these days are very good and quite acceptable to most speech users.

http://thepenguinpodcast.blogs.com/

http://www.penguin.co.uk/static/cs/uk/0/epenguin/index.html

Project Gutenberg

Project Gutenberg is the first and probably still the largest producer of free e-books. There are now over 30,000 titles on this website which, being out of copyright, are free to download and manipulate as needed to make them accessible for students. The books on Project Gutenberg are almost by definition from the canon of mainstream popular classics, but there are often times when a student, either on their own initiative or as part of a class exercise, asks for these texts and because they cannot access the standard print edition for some reason would be stuck were it not for this website.

Works can be accessed through the main catalogue – author or title search, or most recently added. There are works in many languages as well as English, and links to websites offering audio books either with a computer voice (one of their own recent projects), or with human voices, such as Librivox. For instance, searching for Charles Dickens brings up, as well as the texts of all his works, audio files of many of them (it has to be said that listening to *Bleak House* read by a computer is not for the fainthearted!) and a link to the Wikipedia entry for the author. In turn, clicking on the text file brings up a range of options for download, such as a compressed zip file, html, pdf or plain text. Copy and paste from a text file means that the book can then be produced in whatever font and print size is required for the individual student.

This is a really useful website for those providing services for students with disabilities, because it is so accessible and the texts are easy to download. Apart from the obvious classics, there are many short stories and other works of interest such as texts by Darwin and Winston Churchill – it's well worth a browse. Students whose cognitive abilities are average or above but with text impairments would possibly benefit the most from Project Gutenberg, but many others might enjoy it as well.

www.gutenberg.org/wiki/Main_Page

Radio 4 Extra

Radio 4 Extra is the now renamed Radio 7. Although the children's programming has been drastically reduced since the relaunch the emphasis now is on 'family-friendly content'. The website for the show is clearly laid out and easily navigable. Serialised stories feature heavily and change frequently. To illustrate, Ian Serraillier's *The Silver Sword*, Terry Pratchett's *Night Watch*, Alan Garner's *Elidor*, J. G. Ballard's *The Drowned World*, Jane Austen's *Persuasion*, Bill Bryson's *Notes from a Small Island* and L. Frank Baum's *The Wizard of Oz* are scheduled at the time of writing, offering something for every taste and all performed by distinguished and proven actors.

http://www.bbc.co.uk/radio4extra/

Read How You Want

Read How You Want's mission is to 'provide the format of choice for every reader' and formats include Large Print, Supersize editions, DAISY, Braille and e-books. Over 4,000 titles are now available in the UK and, because this is a customised book source, it is possible to specify which point size best suits your readers. UK libraries receive discounts on orders placed through the website and delivery is free.

http://www.readhowyouwant.com/

Rising Stars

Rising Stars is a leading publishing specialist of materials for reluctant and struggling readers including fiction, nonfiction and plays. Many titles can now also be supplied in ePDF format for reading on PCs, netbooks, laptops, tablets, whiteboards and mobile phones.

Their new e-bookshelves offer a range of 12 of their most popular e-book titles grouped together around particular audiences and themes: reluctant boys, reluctant girls, graphic novels, paired reader, sport and teenage reads.

http://www.risingstars-uk.com/

http://www.risingstars-uk.com/all-series/rising-stars-ebookshelves/

Rising Stars Customer Services, PO Box 105, Rochester, Kent, ME2 4BE
custcare@risingstars-uk.com or 0800 091 1602

RNIB

RNIB is a leading sight loss charity and provider of books in accessible formats including DAISY unabridged audiobooks and magazines on CD.

Services now include the National Library for the Blind. The RNIB National Library Service aims to give blind and partially sighted children the same access to library services as those who are sighted. Although there is a subscription fee for talking books, Braille or giant print (Arial Bold 24 point) is free. Although the RNIB Library Service do not currently stock text books or reading schemes they do provide common core texts such as Shakespeare plays and non-fiction topic work books.

The RNIB textbook pilot scheme offers over 100 commonly used electronic textbooks appropriate for students with a print impairment, including dyslexia, for a small charge.

RNIB also produce booklists across various formats as well as a regular magazine, *Read On*, which features a column for children.

www.rnib.org.uk

www.rnib.org.uk/textbooks

www.rnib.org.uk/reading

105 Judd Street, London WC1H 9NE
0303 123 9999
childrenslibrarian@rnib.org.uk or helpline@rnib.org.uk

In addition, RNIB produce an informative leaflet *Ways of Reading: finding books for children and young people who are blind or partially sighted*. The leaflet covers reading material for pleasure, information and school work.

Downloadable from
http://www.rnib.org.uk/livingwithsightloss/Documents/ways_of_reading.pdf

Seeing Ear

The Seeing Ear is an online library providing contemporary and classic fiction and nonfiction books for adults and children in electronic format, for download by registered members of the library. Membership is open to the partially sighted or dyslexic in the UK or EU as well as their teachers and parents. Schools can also become members.

http://www.seeingear.org

> The Seeing Ear, Carolyn House, 383 Battle Road, St Leonards-on-Sea, East Sussex, TN37 7BE
> librarian@seeingear.org

Self-Made Hero

Self-Made Hero is an independent publisher creating sophisticated graphic novel versions of classics, crime, sci-fi, horror, original fiction and manga Shakespeare.

http://www.selfmadehero.com/

> 5 Upper Wimpole Street, London, W1G 6BP
> info@selfmadehero.com or 020 7487 4395

Sound Learning

Sound Learning from Listening Books supports the National Curriculum from KS2 to A level through the provision of set texts and study guides on audio.

http://www.soundlearning.org.uk/

Storynory

Storynory provides free audio stories for kids read by professional actors with a different story being published each week. Choose from Original, Junior, Fairytales, Classic Authors or Educational (myths and legends and catchphrases).

http://storynory.com/

Library Suppliers

Audiobooks and e-books from your library supplier

A number of library suppliers are now trying to capitalise on the rapid increase in e-book reading and audiobook listening. The situation is rapidly changing at the time of going to press so you will need to check supplier websites for current details and pricing. While some are adopting the solutions adopted by US and NZ suppliers others are creating their own platforms.

Dawsonera
http://www.dawsonera.com/

Dawsonera is a major supplier of academic titles to libraries, particularly Universities and Research Institutions. They offer titles from publishers such as CUP, OUP, Blackwells, Routledge and Sage. There is a hosting fee and books are bought and billed individually. Once purchased the library retains permanent ownership of that title even if the hosting fee is no longer paid. It is also possible to 'rent' rather than buy a particular title.

A free trial is available.

JCS Resources
http://www.jcsonlineresources.org/

JCS offers a vast range of online subscription resources aimed at the schools market including e-books, databases, journals and multimedia. Pricing is based on the number of users though generous consortium discounts are available as well as a free trial.

MLS
http://www.microlib.co.uk/home/eBooks.aspx

At the start of 2012 Microlibrarian Systems began to offer an e-book and Audio Library solution powered by Overdrive, one of the main global hosting platforms.

The e-books chosen from an extensive catalogue can be imported to and accessed from Eclipse and Junior Librarian alongside existing library resources. Overdrive supports all leading devices and operating systems including Kobo, Sony, iPod, Android and Blackberry. At present downloading to Kindle is only available in the US.

Pricing structures are dependent on school size.

NetLibrary
http://www.netlibrary.com/

NetLibrary provides e-content solutions for libraries including e-books and audiobooks.

OverDrive

www.overdrive.com

Global distributor of e-books and audiobooks to libraries including schools. Many public library authorities in the UK now use OverDrive for e-book and audio lending. It is worth pointing students towards these extra free resources and working with your public library to promote the e-resources they have available.

Peters ePlatform

http://petersbooks.co.uk/eplatform

Children's book supplier Peters has partnered with Wheelers Books to create a secure, personalised e-lending platform for schools. E-books can be read on a variety of end-user devices and access is through the school's library management system or directly through the online platform. After an initial set-up fee e-books are charged per download or via an annual fee. Access to a demo site is available.

Public Library Online

http://publiclibraryonline.wordpress.com/

PLO for the UK offers concurrent online access to a customisable range of titles. Added extras include reading group guides and author interview videos. School library subscriptions are available.

RM Books

https://www.rmbookshelf.com

RM Books allows schools to select, rent or buy digital textbooks. Enhanced features include embedded video and assessment tools. Once selected, books can be allocated to individual students or whole classes as required. RM books have apps for iOS and Android devices and work with a variety of e-readers. Access codes depend on the time period chosen for each individual title and a substantial range is available for different subjects from the recognised textbook publishers. Any UK educational establishment can register.

VLeBooks

http://www.vlebooks.com/

VLeBooks is a brand new e-book lending platform developed by Browns Books for Students. E-books are tailored to the UK education market and are ordered via Navigator.net, made available to students on a unique website and can be read on a PC or mobile device. There is a one-off set-up fee and an additional annual platform fee. A free trial is available.

Case Study 1

Moira Johnson

Learning Resources Manager, Treloar College, Hampshire

Juliet Leeves

LRC Adviser, Treloar College

Information Access for All at Treloar College

Introduction

Treloar College is a specialist college for young people with physical disabilities aged 16 or over, who come from all parts of the UK and overseas. Based in Holybourne, near Alton in Hampshire, it offers a holistic approach in an educational, therapeutic and residential environment. Co-located with Treloar School, which provides for younger students, it is the largest provider of specialist education in the South East.

Students at Treloar College have a wide spectrum of physical, learning, communication, language and sensory difficulties. The sensory range extends from profound deafness or visual impairment through to lesser levels of loss, which may only be temporary. Other students have multi-sensory difficulties alongside associated physical difficulties and many students have learning difficulties and disabilities, some with profound multiple learning difficulties (PMLD).

All students entering the college have a range of assessments to assist them to select the most appropriate studies. We offer a number of learner pathways dependent on the abilities and achievements of each individual student. These include: an interactive and sensory group, aimed at the more complex disabled and sensory impaired students; creative and enterprise pathways, offered to students working between entry levels 1-3 (pre-GCSE); and vocational studies, both at levels 1 and 2 (within the GCSE range), and at Advanced Level. Further Advanced Level subjects are also available through Treloar's close link with nearby Alton College.

Each student is supported by a dedicated Multi-Disciplinary Team. These teams are based on site, available on-call and tasked to coordinate and support every aspect of the student's education, therapy, care, social and independence skills.

Learning Resources

Learning Resources provides an information and resources service across Treloar College and School. The Learning Resources Centre (LRC), based in College, is the main service hub, and there is also a small School library. In the LRC, we support teaching and learning across College, and also provide extra-curricular support after college in the evenings and at weekends. Literacy support includes running the annual Six Book Challenge as well as one-to-one literacy support sessions. One-to-one support sessions are also offered outside teaching hours, and could be anything from helping with emails to internet shopping. The LRC becomes more of a social space during the evenings and at weekends, with student DJs broadcasting after 4.30pm, and various activities being offered, such as Books Aloud reading club, student magazine and iPad club.

Every student an individual

Learners are treated very much as individuals. Each student has an assessment to identify the technology needed to support them in the classroom, and students have a roving profile which means their configuration follows them around and they can access the software they need on any PC (provided the PC has the relevant software loaded).

The roving profile also ensures that the basic accessibility settings for each student are available on any PC they access. These are agreed with therapists and the Visual Impairment Officer and are standard Windows adjustments. They can include, for example, colour options, font size on menus and type of cursor.

In the LRC, we provide a variety of assistive technology to enable students to work as independently as possible. For example, as well as a standard mouse, we offer joysticks, rollerballs and touchpad mouse. Keyboards come as standard, large and small with or without key guards, and keyboard labels are sometimes used to highlight letters on keyboards for students with a visual impairment (e.g. black lettering on yellow). A variety of different headphones are also provided.

Some students access the PC using switch technology, normally a head switch mounted on their wheelchair headrest and connected to the PC in various ways. LRC staff just have to log the user into the system and then they can work independently, often using an on-screen keyboard such as Click-n-Type. Some modern wheelchairs have Infra-red and Bluetooth connectivity built into the controllers. This means that with a suitable receiver, the wheelchair joystick can control the mouse, providing an ergonomic solution. There are devices that monitor head position to control the mouse and very hi-tech solutions that work by tracking eye movement.

Our Assistive Technology department

The basic software build on our PCs includes Microsoft Outlook, Microsoft Office, Windows Media Player, Internet Explorer, Adobe Reader and TEXTHelp Read&Write Gold (this last is a literacy-based program and is discussed further below, along with other specialised software packages we use.) Along with these packages which are available on all PCs, other standard software includes Microsoft Publisher and FrontPage, Adobe Photoshop and CorelDRAW. Other assistive software can be installed on specific PCs for students if required, subject to licensing conditions.

Assistive software

Read&Write Gold from TEXTHelp is used widely across college to help users with reading and writing difficulties. It includes a screen reader which is used by many of our students, particularly those with a visual impairment. Writing features include word prediction, which displays predicted words in the Prediction window as they are typed. The system can be set up to speak a word if the mouse is hovered over it. The prediction facility can be set up to learn vocabulary patterns for individual users to provide a list of possible words which can be used to finish sentences. Reading features include reading each word out as it is typed, or at the end of a sentence or paragraph.

ZoomText from Ai Squared is used by students with a severe visual impairment. It is a highly functional package which includes both a magnifier and a reader. Within the magnifier function, the magnification required can be selected, and the colour, pointer and cursor can be customised. There are also 'finder' functions for searching the desktop and text. Within the reader function, speech can be enabled or disabled as required. If enabled, the system reads everything, including menu options and actions, not just selected text as with other screen readers. The speech rate can be set and the 'hints' function offers other options such as changing pitch for capital letters.

Dragon Naturally Speaking is a standard commercial package which is not specifically aimed at disabled users but has been used successfully in college for some years. The student wears a headset with microphone and essentially the system types what the student speaks. It associates a sound with a word, so a voice file is built up for each student. Verbal commands can be given, e.g. 'read that', 'full stop', but the student needs to learn how to give commands without pauses so it does not type the individual words. By definition, this system can only be used by students with speech (some of our students are non-verbal) and a degree of cognitive ability, but it has been used effectively to speed up typing for those students who can speak faster than they can type!

EZ Keys is a hardware and software combination built around switch access and using an on-screen keyboard with in-built prediction. This combination reduces time and effort for the user and has been used successfully by a number of our students.

Specialist kit

In addition to the assistive technology used on PCs in the LRC, we have a range of stand-alone devices to support our students. myReader from Humanware is a text magnifier which offers full page document capture onto a built-in 15" LCD screen. Various text layout modes are available, including column, row and word formats, and there is a range of contrasting colour combinations for presenting the text. The reading speed can be set and myReader scrolls the text automatically at that speed; manual scrolling is also available. There is an easy-to-use hand control unit which can be used by many of our students.

We regularly use myReader in our one-to-one literacy support sessions. Staff have liaised with the Literacy tutor on target-setting, and support students in short sessions in the LRC which are sometimes during teaching hours or could be outside the teaching day. We have a range of graded readers from Entry 1 to

Level 2 which are used in these sessions, and the Quick Reads series are also very popular with students.

Other devices for reading print aloud include the Intel Reader, which combines a high resolution camera for capturing the text which is then converted to digital text and read aloud.

We have a Plextalk DAISY Information Player from RNIB for reading DAISY digital talking books (see below) and we also loan ordinary CD players for audio books (models which remember where you left off in a story are particularly helpful!). Our cabinet of equipment for students with a visual impairment holds a large selection of magnifiers of different strengths as well as talking clocks, talking signs and talking calculators.

Alternative formats

Our students' disabilities demand that we provide alternative format materials in whatever format best suits their needs. Resources therefore include a wide range of alternative format material. We have a good collection of large print books in different font sizes, and use the CustomEyes service from the National Blind Children's Society to produce large print books in the required font size. CustomEyes also produce the World Book Day £1 books in large print format for which students can exchange their tokens. We also subscribe to RNIB's weekly Big Print news and TV/Radio guide.

Our large print books can be used for students with a visual impairment requiring help with reading. One of our students who wanted to improve his reading worked with an LRC volunteer who had been trained in effective paired reading. This system allows for the student and trainer to read together or separately as desired by the student, and has been shown to extend the reading experience and improve confidence. Together they read *Harry Potter and the Deathly Hallows* in giant print (which ran to five volumes!)

Audio books are very popular. We hold a stock of commercially produced audio books on CD and also borrow audio books from a variety of sources. Increasingly, audio books are becoming available on a variety of platforms, including streaming direct to the PC and downloading to other devices such as iPad and iPhone.

We also have the EasyConverter software from Dolphin which can convert scanned text or electronic files into large print, DAISY, MP3 audio and braille (although we do not use this last option), allowing us to produce customised alternative format material. We have used this with students reading graded readers who require large print text, scanning in the printed text and producing large print in the required font size.

Resources from other organisations

We use a wide range of organisations to source alternative format material which is not held in stock. Hampshire County Library provide an invaluable inter-library loan service, allowing us to borrow large print and audio books, as well as audio-described DVDs. The mobile library also visits Treloar once a month and has proved popular with the school pupils, although only two wheelchairs at a time can come on board! E-books and audiobooks are also available to download to a variety of devices using the Overdrive digital library. This has potential for our students, but we are still assessing both the content on Overdrive and the process for downloading which has not proved straightforward in our networked environment. This could present some accessibility issues for our students, particularly those with a visual impairment.

The RNIB National Library Service provides a range of services, but our students have to join the RNIB as individuals, and whilst membership is free, some services, like the Talking Book Service which supplies books in the DAISY format, is on a subscription basis, meaning that each of our students has to subscribe individually. DAISY books have a number of advantages over ordinary audio books, as they provide enhanced navigation, allowing the reader to skip sections, jump to certain parts of the text or find a specific page. Publishing in the DAISY format also allows the user to decide how they access the material, for example, only listening to the audio or accessing images and/or text (http://www.rnib.org.uk/livingwithsightloss/readingwriting/Talkingbooksanddaisyplayers). Other RNIB options include the BookStream book club for DAISY books, and large/giant print books to borrow or buy (braille books are also available but we do not have any blind students).

The UK Talking Newspapers Association (TNAUK, now part of RNIB) provides talking newspapers and magazines in a variety of formats including audio CD, audio download, full text and DAISY. We do not currently subscribe to this service although we have done in the past. As with the other RNIB services, students have to subscribe individually to this service.

We also use other suppliers of audio books include Calibre and Listening Books, both of which offer a range of options for delivery of audio books.

Textbooks in alternative formats

Students who are visually or print impaired (i.e. cannot hold a book) may require textbooks in alternative formats, e.g. large print, audio or electronic format for reading on screen using assistive technology. It is possible that the title may already be available commercially in digital format (as an e-book), or an alternative format may already exist, e.g. from the RNIB National Library Service. Otherwise, it will be necessary to obtain the textbook from the publisher in an electronic format which can be used to produce a suitable alternative format for the student.

It is always best to plan in advance if textbooks in alternative formats are likely to be necessary. LRC staff liaise with tutors and students on access needs and likely book needs and agree on the best format for particular titles. We can advise on costs (if any) and agree who pays if there is a cost. We can then identify if a title is available commercially, and whether it can be bought or borrowed.

If the title is not already available in an alternative format to buy or borrow, it may be possible to obtain an electronic copy from the publisher. JISC TechDis has produced a useful guide to this process (http://goo.gl/y0xK9) from which we have developed our own procedures which involve the following stages:

- Contact the publisher: Permissions Department is best, or Customer Services. TechDis have worked with the Publishers Association to create Publisher Lookup UK, a useful online database in which this information can be found (www.publisherlookup.org.uk).

- Provide standard book details, e.g. author, title, ISBN, publication date.

- Ask for a PDF version of the book. This should have selectable text (i.e. not an image of the text) and ideally be marked up for structure and reading order.

- Depending on the licence conditions, the publisher may require the name of the student. As there may be data protection issues here, it is important to ascertain how this data will be used. It is also important that the student gives his/her permission to release this information and understands what he/she is agreeing to, and that you record this fact.

- Find out if any costs are involved – if the student already has a copy of the book, there may be no cost.

- When the file is received, pass to the student's tutor together with the licence and ensure both are aware of the licence conditions.

We have successfully used these procedures to obtain text books for a print impaired student. This student used switch technology to access information on a PC, but had to rely on his LSA sitting by him and turning the pages of any hard copy material. It only took a few days to get the PDF file which the student could access independently on a PC whenever he wished. We were most impressed with the publisher (Nelson Thornes) whom we nominated for the TechDis Publisher Lookup Award for Library Service which recognises publishers whose responsiveness to requests brings significant benefits to disabled learners (http://www.jisctechdis.ac.uk/techdis/pages/detail/floating_pages/PLU_PR).

The future is digital?

The digital revolution has meant that increasingly our students are able access the information they require in digital form via a PC or other electronic device such as a tablet. We have a large number of iPads which are widely used across both College and School (we have also purchased robust cases in case they are dropped!). We also have Kindle e-book readers, RM Slate and Android devices. Accessibility varies between devices, but it is probably fair to say the iPad offers the best range of options, with accessibility settings including voiceover (reads whatever is on the screen), speech selection (for selected text) and assistive touch (allowing multi-touch gestures with a single finger and adaptive input devices such as switches). The RM Slate, being Windows-based, also offers the possibility of using the assistive technology required by some of our students, including switch technology.

The e-reading devices we use offer the ability to change font size and colour reversal (white on black), together with zoom and speech functions, which are particularly useful for learners with a visual impairment, although the computer-generated voices used for e-books do not offer the same listening experience as an audio book! The recent TechDis Voices initiative offers two new high-quality, youthful and modern voices (TechDis Jack and TechDis Jill) which can be used with text-to-speech tools and are available to all learners over 16 in every publicly-funded learning provider in England (www.jisctechdis.ac.uk/voices).

E-books and e-audio books have great potential for our students, whether read on a PC or one of our other devices. However, the options available vary, depending both on the functionality of the book downloaded and the app used. Many e-books are also not at an appropriate level for learners on Entry Level or Level 1; however, interactive or augmented reality books can be particularly useful for students with a sensory impairment or learning disability.

Whilst digital information potentially widens the range of options available to our students, having information in digital form does not necessarily mean that it is accessible. This has been recognised by TechDis who are managing a new service to convert digital information into accessible formats for the benefit of learners who have difficulty reading or understanding text on PCs or mobile devices. MyDocStore will allow users to access all forms of digital resources according to their preferred format (www.mydocstore.org.uk). The service can change digital information into different fonts, colours, or styles as well as provide an audio version or accessible e-books. TechDis also offer a useful toolbox to help users adapt the technology they use everyday, such as Windows, tablets and mobile phones (www.jisctechdis.ac.uk/tbx).

At Treloar, our emphasis on the individual learner means that we will continue to offer resources in whatever format is most helpful to any particular student and on whatever device is best suited to them. The digital age allows us to expand our services, whilst retaining the wealth of resources we already offer.

Note: The legal requirements for the use and loan of audiobooks, e-books and e-readers in libraries vary, so please consult the terms and conditions of your supplier. For further information, see the e-resources page in the Support for Secondary Schools section of the SLA website: www.sla.org.uk/eresources.php

Shona Phillips

Librarian, The Edinburgh Academy, Edinburgh (previously, Librarian, Royal Blind School, Edinburgh)

School Library Provision for Children and Young People with Special Needs

Introduction

I have worked in school libraries for over 12 years now, mainly in the Special Needs (SEN) sector, working with children and young people with a wide variety of specific educational and physical needs. Although a novice when I began, I have found this one of the most rewarding parts of my career thus far. I felt doubly honoured when the School Library Association (SLA) not only placed me on their Honour List for School Librarian of the Year in 2008 but also awarded me a special award in recognition of my work with SEN students.

Over the years I have always felt that it would be great to have a starting point, not a specific 'how to' guide, but examples of what has been done before. Crucially, as with all other aspects of school library provision, one size does not fit all. But here are some examples of projects I have run over the years with varying groups of SEN students.

Access all areas

Your audience is a key factor when working with children and young people with SEN. Not only do you have to deal with the standard reading challenges all pupils present, but their additional needs have to be taken into consideration.

The simplest starting point is access. Do your students have mobility issues or a visual or hearing impairment? Crucially, is your school library accessible to all students in school. Ideally the floor space should be kept as clear as possible and the layout of the library, including free standing displays, left stationary. This enables students to learn the layout of the library and become comfortable moving around it independently.

This is also true for the collections; students will quickly learn where they expect resources to be. Clear displays and shelf labelling help in this situation. One of the biggest challenges I have often faced is changing any of the above. Change is often a huge challenge for many SEN pupils and although as librarians we strive to keep the space dynamic and interesting it is worth keeping in mind that even the minutest of changes might have a dramatic effect on whether that student is comfortable coming back into the library. On more than one occasion I have had a student refuse to enter because I've moved a floor spinner, or changed the displays without warning them.

As well as physical layout, what is in your collections is also important. There are now a wide variety of alternative formats available, from Braille and large print to audio and digital publishing. Over the years I have found the best way to get students through the door is to remove their most common complaint, 'you won't have anything I can read, Miss!' Adapting the collections to the students rather than the other way round is the easiest way of persuading them across the threshold. Finding out the way in which the students access print before they come to school is always the ideal, but with the best will in the world that isn't always going to happen. Nowadays however suppliers have a fast turn around and you are rarely waiting for more than a week for even the more complex alternative formats, such as Braille.

Book Club

Book clubs are an integral part of many school libraries and I felt it was an experience our students would benefit from. Many of our students had never participated in such an event before, so a shadowing group for the Carnegie Medal was initially set up and our book group grew from there.

Our philosophy was the same as many other school book groups – to encourage a love of reading. I just had to be a little more prepared. I had to consider the range of needs within my group, ranging from behaviour strategies – i.e. did this pupil have a behaviour plan and exit strategy if required – to physical and print access. All of these often necessitated meetings with the support staff assisting the pupils. Preparing in this manner meant that when the pupils came along to book club we were able to concentrate on discussing books; they also appeared more relaxed and willing to participate, as some of the barriers had been removed.

The book club went from strength to strength and its success meant that it became an integral part of the curriculum for each year group who had a timetabled session in the library throughout the school year.

Information Literacy

As well as the book clubs, information literacy courses for primary and secondary pupils were also a key part of my remit. Again preparation was the key, however I now had to consider alternative technologies as well as alternative formats. Technologies such as literacy software for dyslexic pupils to magnification and screen reading software for those pupils with a visual impairment. Using these technologies is the way in which many SEN pupils access the internet and other desktop packages, so it was crucial that the information literacy course ran through these packages instead of merely acknowledging them.

An effective example of this was an S2 (Year 9) information literacy lesson on evaluating search engines. Within my secondary group that year I had two pupils using screen reading software, one pupil using magnification software and three pupils using a dictation package. The exercises attributed to the lesson had to run smoothly through all these packages, so that all the pupils ended up at the same point by the end of the lesson. The pupils were split into groups and those using the alternative packages deliberately split up. All of our groups managed to compare several search engines and make a presentation to the rest of the class on which they would recommend. Interestingly both the groups which had the pupils using the screen reading software made the computer read their presentation.

E-books and E-readers

The developments in the digital publishing world have been avidly watched by those working in SEN. E-publishing and access to books in electronic formats opens up numerous possibilities in providing alternative access to literacy for SEN students.

E-readers have been a great addition to the library – I stock Kindles and iPads, both of which have the capability of altering text size, background and font colour and can, with the use of a synthesised voice, read the page in front of them at the touch of button. Books that often took weeks to translate into an alternative format are now available at the same time as their standard counterparts. Great examples of these are *Twilight* and *The Hunger Games* series.

However, at the opposite end of the literacy spectrum these devices have really benefited many of our pupils, who struggle with reading. I've found these pupils are much more willing to sit in class or the library and read a book on an e-reader as opposed to its printed counterpart, as no one can see what they're reading. Crucially for SEN pupils, they can comfortably enjoy the experience of reading a book without worrying about what their friends are going to say.

I will continue to watch the developments in this field avidly as I feel it is going to be a very effective literacy tool to use with children and young people with SEN.

Conclusion

These are some of the examples and strategies I have used over the years, Working with children and young people with SEN is never an exact science and the most important lesson I have learned is that children and young people with SEN simply want to be the same as everyone else and if I can remove some of the barriers that they so often face when accessing education and pass on a love and appreciation of literacy then I feel I have achieved my goal.

Note: The legal requirements for the use and loan of audiobooks, e-books and e-readers in libraries vary, so please consult the terms and conditions of your supplier. For further information, see the e-resources page in the Support for Secondary Schools section of the SLA website: www.sla.org.uk/eresources.php

Case Study 3

Claire Larson

Hursthead Junior School, Stockport

Using E-readers for a Book Group
at a Junior School

Those Neil Armstrong Moments...

There's something special about being a pioneer and I still remember the occasion over twenty years ago when I experienced the internet for the very first time. It was a rainy lunch hour and the school library was buzzing. A crowd of students gathered around one of our state of the art LRC computers. The modem blinked and beeped and with the solemnity of Deep Thought and the speed of an arthritic lawnmower we connected to the World Wide Web. The atmosphere was electric, the students jubilant and we all felt part of something special. This was our Neil Armstrong moment and although it was almost a quarter of a century ago, some of those students will probably still remember the significance of the occasion.

Of course it is exciting to be at the cutting edge and with the pace of technological change ever faster, young people today are often trail blazers, experiencing the excitement and drama of innovative technology on a regular basis.

The junior school where I work is situated in the leafy suburbs of Stockport. We are a book loving school where reading is high on the agenda, with numerous author visits, a programme to shadow the annual Stockport Schools' Book Award and an enthusiastic team of Year 6 librarians. We work hard to develop reading confidence and fluency, especially for those who need extra support and we aim to foster a universal enthusiasm for books, authors and reading. Meeting these aims while tapping into current technology made e-readers an obvious choice for our newly formed book group.

Starting Up – The NOT Kindle Club!

E-books have seen a huge growth in popularity and often feature in the media. A growing number of our pupils own their own e-reader and are enthusiastic about their versatility. School had already purchased a set of e-readers and we felt that using them for our book group would be convenient, fun and an opportunity to trial an evolving technology.

We decided that the focus for our group would be able Year 6 children who would relish a challenging read, and the book group was promoted as a voluntary lunchtime club; children would borrow an e-reader, read the book in their own time and attend a lunchtime session to discuss the book through games and debate. We had no shortage of volunteers and sixteen children were keen to join. More girls than boys volunteered and we set up two groups, each with five girls and three boys.

The children were enthusiastic about borrowing the e-readers and initially I was grilled more about the e-readers than the choice of books: 'How much did it cost?' 'Can I use it at school?' 'Can I download my own books?' 'Does the battery need charging?' 'How do you turn the pages?' This preoccupation was understandable and I reminded myself of that Neil Armstrong moment all those years ago when the pupils were more fixated about the mechanics of linking to the internet than the information they would be able to access. However, we feel it is vital to treat the e-reader as the tool, so, if any children talk about 'The Kindle Club' we gently, but firmly correct them – it is a book group; the e-reader is the means to an end, and the book group is all about enjoying a good read.

Accident Alerts!

Running a Book Group with e-books means purchasing expensive hardware, but as the e-readers operate on a single account we only have to buy one copy of a book, as it can be downloaded quickly and easily to all the e-readers. This saves money in the long term and means we can trial a book inexpensively before copying it across all e-readers. Protecting the hardware is a priority, so e-reader covers have been purchased too.

Young children don't often think about consequences and bearing in mind the impulsive, carefree nature of the average ten and eleven year old we have had very few 'incidents'. There have been inevitable accidents with leaky water bottles and burst yoghurts, but as the e-readers are protected by their cover and then stored in a waterproof folder no damage has been caused. An e-reader was mislaid in the cloakroom before being located under someone's swimming kit and we have our fair share of greasy finger marks and biscuit crumbs, but at least I don't have to grumble about corners of pages being folded down as a book mark! The e-readers are proving robust and the children are so enthusiastic about belonging to the book group that they do take great care of them.

The Best Bits

Having this electronic tool at our finger tips has proved useful. One of the Book Group members has a visual impairment. When in class all reading material has to be enlarged, which means she is often handling unwieldy A3 photocopies while her classmates are reading from ordinary texts. Using the e-reader means that during Book Group she can alter the text size herself (and that element of control increases independence) and she is also using exactly the same material as everyone else.

We decided that as each child is borrowing expensive equipment a home/school e-reader agreement is essential. This deals with the importance of looking after the hardware, and the responsibilities for safeguarding. All members of the group and their parents sign to agree that they will not download material of their own on to the e-reader and that they are responsible for its care and safe return.

It's hard to say whether the technology alone has encouraged children to join the book group. All the members were already keen and ambitious readers, although a surprising bonus has been that brothers and sisters have picked up the e-reader at home because of the novelty value. One girl reported back: 'Mum and Dad are always trying to get my brother to read but he never finishes a book. I told him how good *Tribes* was and he started reading it straight away. He loved the e-reader and said it was much easier than reading a book.'

The boy's parents went on to buy him other books by Catherine MacPhail, but in paperback, and when I talked to him, he was enjoying those too. Perhaps the combination of enticing technology and the all important 'right book for the right child' element helped to kick-start the reading habit.

It's easy, Miss... let me show you how

I think we've all experienced those niggles with new technology that a young child seems to solve so effortlessly. Many children appear to have a natural aptitude for technology and whenever I wrestle with something on my mobile phone my twelve year old nephew can sort it out instantly. The members of the book group truly enjoyed my (inflated) sense of helplessness in the face of a stubborn, unresponsive e-reader – they loved showing me how to find a particular page, how to use the dictionary, how to toggle back and forth between pages or chapters and of course how to alter the size of the text – and I did enjoy devouring a whole book without needing my glasses!

The Glitches

The negatives have been few and far between. Handing out and collecting in the e-readers is time consuming. Issuing a library book takes seconds, but ticking off lists for who has which e-reader and who needs a computer charger or a mains charger is more arduous, but definitely worth it.

One of the surprising negatives has been that the children do miss the physical presence of the book that we are going to read. While adults may browse online retailers and look at covers and read blurbs before downloading to their e-reader, the first sight the children had of our chosen books was on the e-reader itself and for our first three downloads no front cover seemed to be available. Judging by the questions on e-reader discussion groups we are not the only people to experience this problem. Lack of a blurb was also a disappointment. For instance, when I announced that we would be reading *The Tulip Touch* some pupils made faces – 'Oh is it about flowers? That sounds a bit boring.' Fortunately I had a hard copy of the book and could show them the dark (physically and metaphorically) front cover and read aloud the blurb which certainly whetted their appetites. I now make a point of having hard copies to hand so that I can share these essential elements of a book. I'm sure this issue will be addressed in the not too distant future.

Tribes proved our most popular choice and I was keen for the Book Group to read others by Catherine MacPhail. Some group members met the author during the glitzy Stockport Schools' Book Award celebration evening (just think BAFTAs for books) and that inspired them even further. Unfortunately at the time no other titles by Catherine MacPhail were available in e-book format. But, again this is an area that will hopefully be resolved as e-books become more widespread.

All the children wanted to know the length of each of our books and enjoyed handling the physical book and flicking through it before heading off happily with their e-readers. E-readers do not tell you what page you are up to, just the percentage you have read and some children found this difficult to get used to, although I grew accustomed to being stopped in the corridor and told 'I'm 50% through...' and 'I've only got 10% left' or 'I read 20% last night!' Some group members were concerned about recording their reading in their reading diaries as their teachers expect them to write the page number they are up to – not possible with an e-book. And what might sound mundane to us does loom large on a young child's horizon, especially when they are used to following very specific rules.

One of the negatives for me was not being able to bookmark pages for discussion. While preparing the sessions I used a hard copy of each book and lots of post-its covered in notes stuck all over the pages. Again, perhaps this is something that will be addressed as e-books become more widely used in education. The potential is certainly there.

The meetings themselves are hugely enjoyable. Our initial choice of books reflected the theme of good versus evil and we chose to read *Tribes* by Catherine MacPhail, *The Tulip Touch* by Anne Fine and *Thief* by Malorie Blackman. The children grew increasingly adept at locating areas of the book they wanted to discuss and even quoting passages. Because we had all three books at our finger tips much of the discussion about *The Tulip Touch* also focused on characters from *Tribes* and in turn from *Thief*, which added depth to the discussions and introduced those ever important higher order reading skills of analysis and comparison. I thought it would be unwieldy to plough through the e-book trying to find specific passages, but the children enjoyed the challenge and many had a natural flair, competing with each other to see who could find the right place first. They certainly knew the books inside out.

Logging Off – last thoughts

It's hard to measure the success of a book group. It's one of those subjective projects where you experience the positives through the feeling of drive and enthusiasm within the group or the perceptive response from a child who is voicing deeply felt opinions. These children are already able and enthusiastic readers, but I am convinced that using the e-reader as a tool enriches their experience. They feel they are at the cutting edge – savouring their own Neil Armstrong moments. They are proud to be using e-readers, enjoy the envy of their friends and put 100% into taking part.

Our next plan is to start up a book group for able but reluctant readers in Year 5. It will be interesting to see whether the e-book element is a driving force and carries through to enjoying the books themselves. Watch this space!

Note: The legal requirements for the use and loan of audiobooks, e-books and e-readers in libraries vary, so please consult the terms and conditions of your supplier. For further information, see the e-resources page in the Support for Secondary Schools section of the SLA website: www.sla.org.uk/eresources.php